DONALD McCULLIN

Mark Haworth-Booth

DONALD

THE GREAT PHOTOGRAPHERS
McCULLIN

COLLINS

DONALD McCULLIN

by Mark Haworth-Booth

Donald McCullin, 1980

'One cannot look at this' was the title Spanish painter Goya inscribed beneath a plate in *The Disasters of War* (1810–13), yet he etched his plates with every intention of publishing them—to record, remember and honour his fallen countrymen, and to make a little money. Few pictures raise such lethal questions of propriety as those of Donald McCullin. Talking about them as one might about other kinds of picture seems all wrong. We are not simply appreciating the excellent photography, but having to cope with the enormity of what the images show. By deliberately choosing to photograph scenes of horror and human tragedy and by confronting the viewer with an unequivocal account of what people can do to one another, McCullin is consciously provoking a reaction—one in which we are all left to deal with on our own.

A decade after McCullin had established himself as a war photographer, the ranks of photojournalists had swelled at a prodigious rate and their conduct in getting their pictures became increasingly aggressive. These tactics were never McCullin's way and, as the renowned journalist and former editor of *Picture Post,* Sir Tom Hopkinson, said of McCullin's photographs, 'They demand a three-fold responsibility: on the part of the photographer, on the part of the editor, on the part of the public.'

Donald McCullin was born in 1935 in St Pancras, London and grew up in Finsbury Park, a working-class district in north London. The family was poor. McCullin's father was a chronic asthmatic and seldom able to work. McCullin described his childhood with reckless honesty in an afterword to his book, *Home-coming.* 'I can smell poverty. It smells like a floor-cloth that's never been washed except in the dirt from the floor it tries to clean.' He added, 'All you were told was based on envy, confusion, and self-pity with a heavy overlay of ignorance.' He was packed off to uncaring households as part of wartime evacuation. Back in London and at the local Secondary Modern school he showed some promise at drawing and won a Trade Art Scholarship to Hammersmith School of Arts and Crafts at the age of 14. He watched his father dying slowly. 'I was angry with God, if he exists, when my father died. I felt that he'd taken a liberty taking my father's life. He was the one person in my life that made the misery of my poverty irrelevant. I mean, it wasn't important, I had my father there every day to see and sit next to . . . I thought I would disown God' (from a BBC interview with Edward Lucie-Smith in 1980). 'I became strong on the very pity I was beginning to feel for myself.'

When his father died in 1950 McCullin left art school and went to work. From the vantage point of his job in a railway restaurant car 'I often had the desire to jump from the train into a river from a great height: I tossed the odd tea-plate out, just to get the feeling of its flying through the air'. Then he worked for two years as a messenger at W.M. Larkins film animation studio in Mayfair, followed by National Service in the RAF. Hoping for an easy life, he opted for darkroom work, printing aerial reconnaissance photographs and photostating maps. He was stationed in Oxfordshire, the Suez Canal Zone, Kenya and Cyprus. He rejoined Larkins in 1956 and in the period which followed he ran with a local gang in Finsbury Park and brushed with the law over brawling incidents.

He bought his first camera, a 6×6 cm ($2\frac{1}{4} \times 2\frac{1}{4}$ inch) twin lens reflex Rolleicord, in 1958 and made snaps of his friends in the gang, which went by the name The Governors, or more properly, The Guv'nors. The gang was involved in the murder of a policeman at the hands of a rival gang. A colleague at Larkins saw some potential news value in McCullin's pictures and acting on the suggestion McCullin found encouragement at *The Observer* newspaper. His first picture story, 'Guv'nors of the Seven Sisters Road', was published by *The Observer* on 15 February 1959. This led to assignments for *The News Chronicle* and *The Sunday Graphic*: 'The People of Tiger Bay', 'Teenage Millionaires: the big spend', 'The Wild Ones' (teenage motorcyclists). Then he pawned his camera to buy a motorbike. His mother had to retrieve it from the pawnshop. In 1961 he married; was sacked by Larkins; went on his own initiative—and with his last £30—to Berlin to photograph the hot story of the building of the Berlin Wall. His pictures were published by *The Observer* and later won a press photography award.

McCullin's professional career blossomed with the arrival in the early sixties of new outlets for photography. Under the art direction of Tom Wolsey, the fashion magazine *Man About Town* became a high quality general magazine (dropping the *'Man About'*). *Town* published McCullin stories on the East End, Finsbury Park, Mayfair, pop music, musclemen and ballet critic Richard Buckle, using new writers like Eric Newby, Geoffrey Cannon and Jeremy Sandford. The quality newspapers launched their colour magazines: *The Sunday Times Magazine* (under Mark Boxer) in 1962, followed by *The Observer* and the *Daily Telegraph* two years later. The photographer Bryn Campbell arrived at *The Observer*'s picture desk in 1964 and put McCullin on a two days a week contract. Campbell brought a fresh excitement and sense of mission into British photography.

When Campbell selected pictures for a British issue of the Swiss magazine *Camera* in June 1963 he made the first written assessment of McCullin: 'His early work was dominated by the subjects he had lived with and knew best—youth gangs, racial minorities, working class life a weekly wage-packet away from poverty. Violence of any kind still fascinates him, perhaps because of his own basic feelings of insecurity. He has already turned out a powerful coverage of the recent brutal Fascist riots in London and he is fretting for an assignment to one of the world's trouble spots. Even his print quality reflects this undercurrent of violence that never seems too deeply submerged in his most typical work. He makes bold use of strong contrast, using tonal extremes to emphasize emotional ones. He is the only young British photo-journalist with a marked, individual style. The straightforward, direct honesty of his work; its underlying emotional strength and visual power, make Don McCullin the most exciting and promising talent in British photography.'

McCullin began to meet other freelance photographers of his generation. On the advice of Philip Jones Griffiths he abandoned the Rolleicord in favour of a single lens reflex camera of 35 mm format. The trusty Rolleicord belonged to the family of cameras used so effectively by Bill Brandt and Brassaï in the 1930s and 40s but was hardly right for action shots: it was held at chest height, the image on the ground glass was laterally transposed, the format was square and the lens was not interchangeable. McCullin acquired a secondhand Pentax. It had the immediate advantages of lightness, use at eye-level and the capacity to take a variety of lenses. With this equipment McCullin left for his first war assignment—to Cyprus in February 1964.

Cyprus was of particular interest to Britain because of its strategic importance and its status as a colony from 1914 to 1960. It was admitted to the Commonwealth as an independent nation in 1961. The divisions between the Greek majority and

Even his print quality reflects this undercurrent of violence that never seems too deeply submerged in his typical work.

the Turkish minority resulted in a long history of violence. Talks on the future of the island broke down in London on 21 January 1964 and vicious street fighting broke out a few weeks later.

McCullin's first pictures from the island were published in *The Observer* on 16 February with this report from Ivan Yates in Nicosia: 'The street fighting in Limassol last week was furtive and ruthless. Well-armed Greeks surrounded the small Turkish community and opened fire from corners and rooftops. Donald McCullin was the only photographer inside the besieged Turkish quarter. He had spent the night in a community centre converted into a hospital and woke on Thursday to the sound of bullets smashing the ironwork outside his window. Old people strayed into the open; combatants stayed warily under cover.' By syndicating the pictures successfully, Campbell was able to send McCullin back to Cyprus twice more in the following weeks. *Paris Match* published McCullin's picture of a Turkish gunman running from the doorway of a cinema (page 24), only they printed it in convincing colour after hand-tinting it. This and other photographs employ the rectangular 35 mm format eloquently. The tragic photograph (pages 26–27) of the grief of a Turkish woman whose husband had just been murdered includes a child who reaches up—as Harold Evans put it—'as much to give as to demand comfort'. McCullin's pictures of Cyprus were seen around the world. He was awarded the Warsaw Gold Medal and the World Press Photographer Award.

Talking to Bryn Campbell in later years McCullin described the risks he had to take in these early assignments: 'At first I had a total disregard for what was flying around. There was nothing I was afraid of, I used to take enormous risks. I wanted to become known in photography. I wanted to open doors that would normally be closed for me.'

McCullin is usually called a war photographer but, from the mid-sixties on, his career took him to many parts of the world on many kinds of assignment not to do with combat. The output of the pioneer photojournalists of the 1920s and 30s seems meagre compared to the jet-age photojournalist McCullin became. His work at this period was distributed through Camera Press in London and his home markets were *The Observer Magazine*, the *Daily Telegraph Magazine* and from 1966 *The Sunday Times Magazine*. McCullin's first assignment for *The Sunday Times Magazine* was an extensive colour story on the Mississippi in 1966. Many more were to follow. McCullin had a brief spell with the Magnum agency in 1967 but was never comfortable with the terms of work and reverted to his freelance role until he took a contract with *The Sunday Times* in 1969. Over the years that followed he worked closely with the magazine's art director and managing editor Michael Rand and designer David King (there 1965–73). In this boom period McCullin's stories were printed with lavish production and at extraordinary length. The designers were able to keep McCullin's pictures away from intrusive advertising—such page spreads are no longer economically feasible.

Although much of McCullin's work was of a mild and domestic nature—like 'Goodbye to the Puff Puffs' (on steam engines) in 1965—or to do with entertainment—his colour portrait of the Beatles for *Life* in 1968—after Cyprus he was immediately in demand for war assignments. In 1964 he was off to Vietnam for the first time and went to the Congo to report on the activities of white mercenary soldiers at Stanleyville. His pictures record this period of civil terror all too clearly

continued on page 57

'There was nothing I was afraid of,' said McCullin. 'I wanted to become known in photography.'

6

THE PHOTOGRAPHS

The graveyard at Haworth, Yorkshire, home of the Brontë sisters, 1967

Collector of death, London, 1962

Sheep on the way to be slaughtered, London, 1961

Steelworker on early shift, Hartlepool, 1963

Collecting coal, Sunderland, 1964

Dead bird, Hertfordshire, 1972

Scarborough, 1967

Down-and-out, London, 1973

Sleeping down-and-out, London, 1973

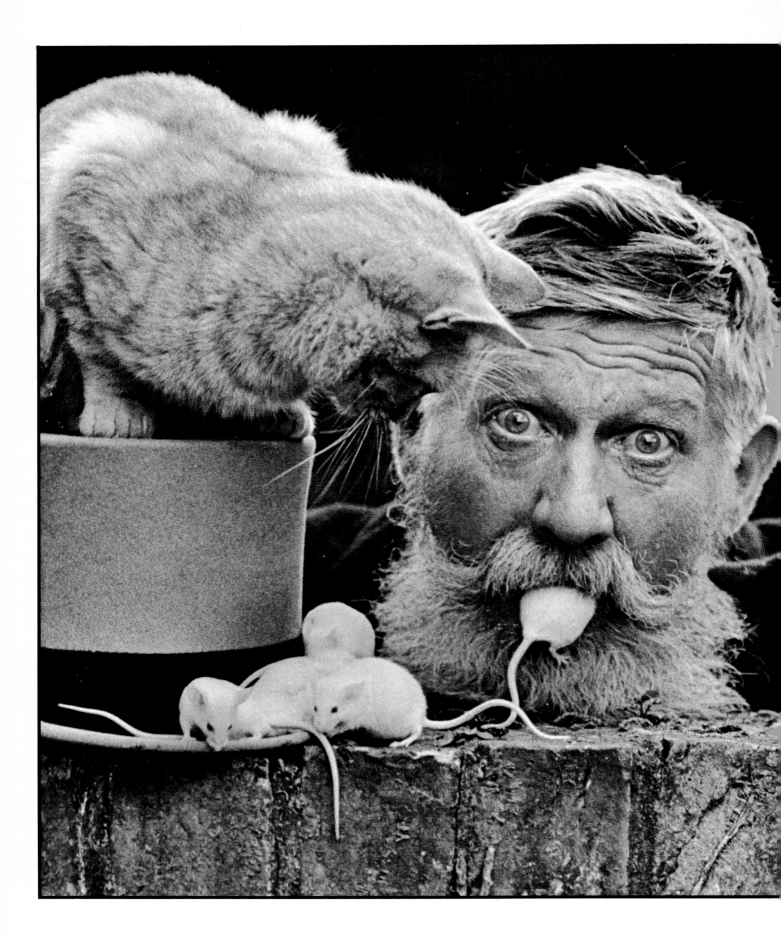

Snowy, the Mouse Man, Cambridge, 1978

Consett steel-works, 1978

Bradford, 1978

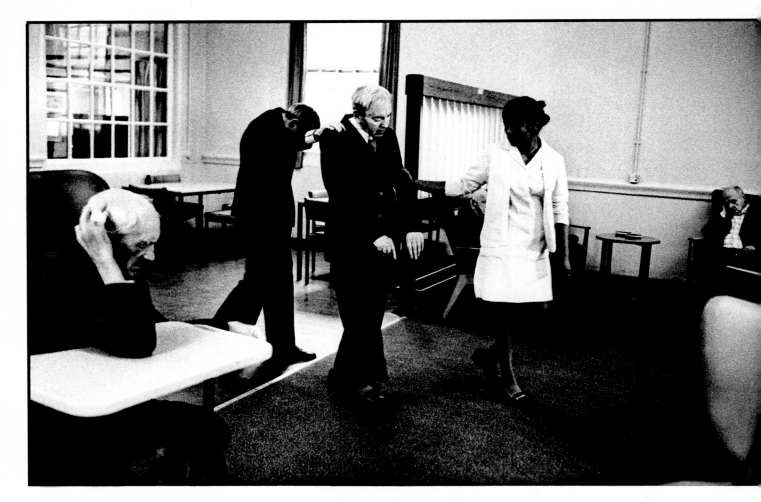

Friern hospital, London, 1978

Stripper in pub, Bradford, 1978

Bradford, 1978

Bradford, 1978

Street fighting, Limassol, Cyprus, 1964

Old man's body dragged away after being shot, Limassol, 1964

Street fighting, Limassol, 1964

Street fighting, Limassol, 1964

Turkish woman discovers bodies of her husband and his brother
killed by Greeks in Cyprus civil war, 1964

Israeli soldiers under heavy fire as they capture the old city of Jerusalem, 1967

Grief-stricken woman and son after husband murdered, Cyprus, 1964 (preceding pages)

Biafran soldier and wounded comrade, 1969

Battle-fatigued Biafran officer talking to dead soldier, 1969

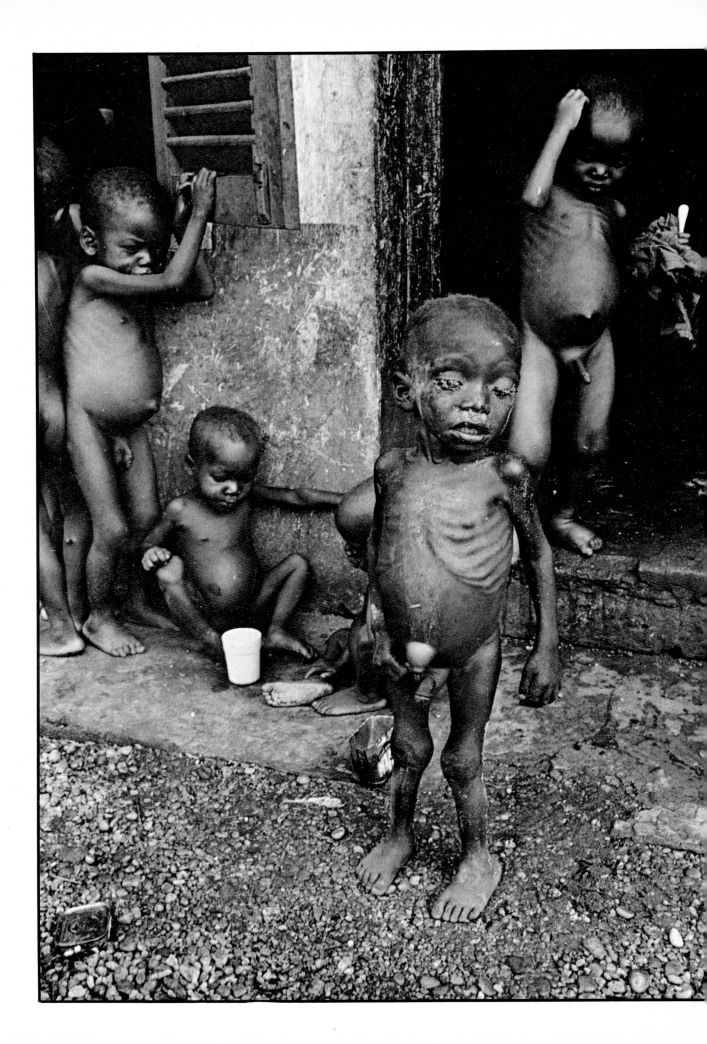

Mentally-handicapped youth begging for food, Biafra, 1969

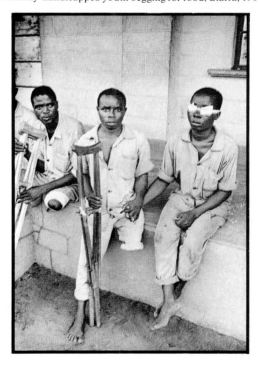

Wounded soldiers, Biafra, 1969

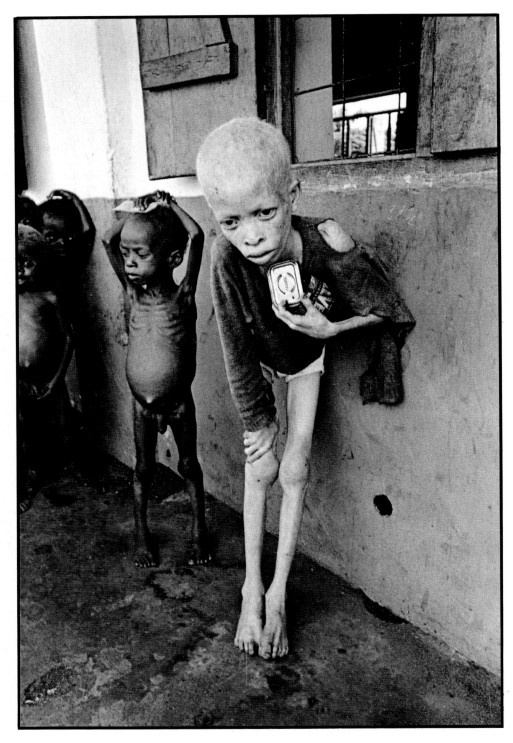

Starving albino boy, Biafra, 1970

24-year-old mother and baby, Biafra, 1969

U.S. Marines with wounded comrade, Hué, 1968

U.S. Marine throwing hand grenade, Hué, 1968

U.S. Marine medic treats dying soldier, Hué, 1968

Injured Vietnamese civilian, Hué, 1968

U.S. chaplain carries old Vietnamese woman to safety, Hué, 1968

Dying U.S. Marine being rushed to field hospital, Hué, 1968

Wounded U.S. Marine dragged to safety, Hué, 1968

Dead Vietnamese soldier, Hué, 1968

Wounded child being rescued by army medic, Hué, 1968

Dying Cambodian soldier, 1970

Cambodian anti-tank gunners in action, Praveng, 1970

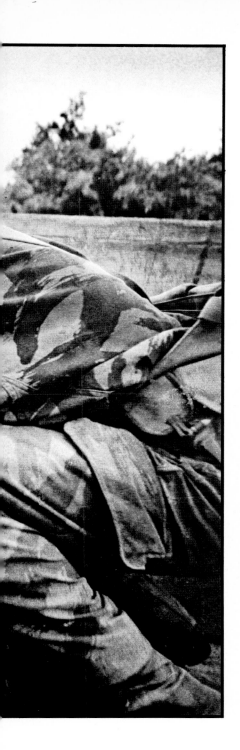

Dead Khmer Rouge soldiers, Praveng, 1970

43

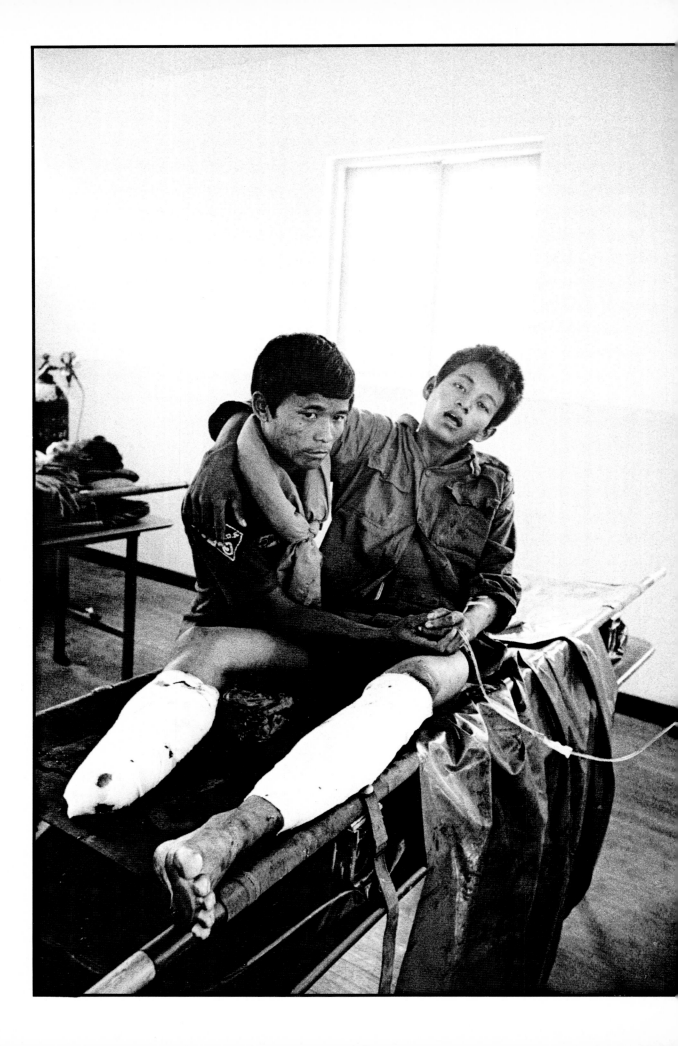

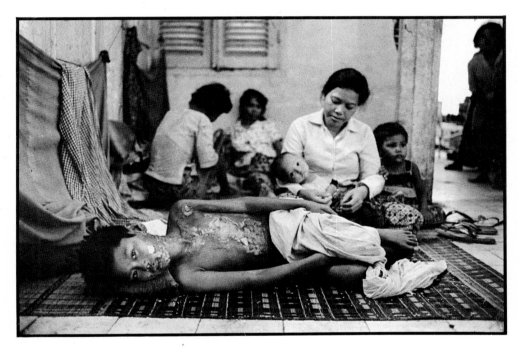

9-year-old napalm victim, Cambodia, 1976

Refugees from Bangladesh in monsoon rains, Indian border, 1971

British soldiers and prisoner, Londonderry, N. Ireland, 1970

Cholera victim being taken to hospital, Bangladesh, 1971

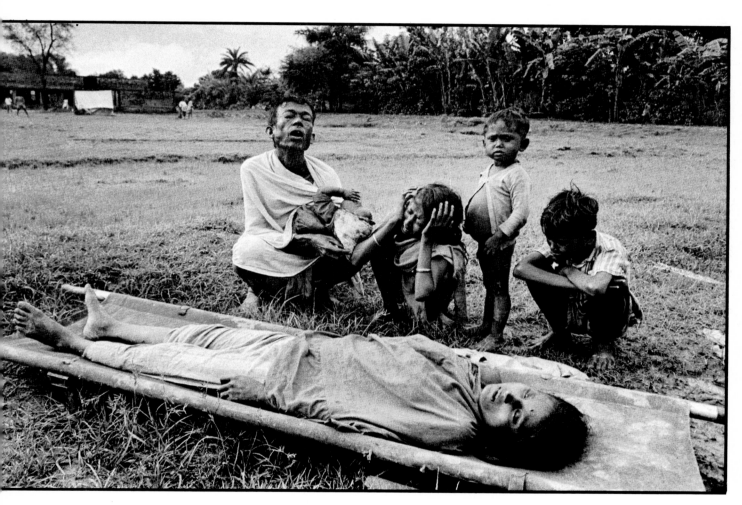

A woman has just died of cholera and her family grieves, Bangladesh, 1971

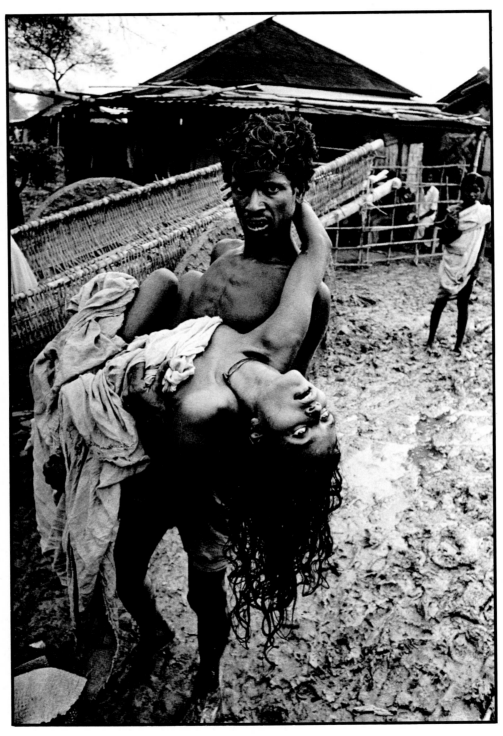

Man and sick wife, probably cholera victim, Bangladesh, 1971

Christian militia mock the body of a young Palestinian girl killed in the battle of Karantina, Beirut, 1976

continued from page 6

but it is worth mentioning that McCullin has often reported with words. His Congo report appeared in *The Observer* as 'Climb aboard for Stanleyville', but was credited to John Gale. McCullin's name was not used so that he could return.

McCullin and his work became particularly established in the minds of a large public through his photographs of the Vietnam war. He visited South Vietnam regularly after 1964 but his crucial work dates from the Tet Offensive of February 1968. McCullin was due to photograph at Khe Sanh but when the offensive was begun by the North on 30 January he diverted to Hué, the old Imperial capital of Vietnam and a city of extreme strategic importance. Hué had been overrun by North Vietnamese troops. The battle which followed was among the most fiercely contested of the war. Civilians were trapped between the opposing forces. McCullin was attached to a company of U.S. Marines during two weeks of fighting during which the citadel was retaken. Losses were severe. As the fighting drew to a close, McCullin withdrew to Saigon where Fred Emery, a correspondent from the London *Times,* took down his story. It appeared on the paper's front page on 23 February.

McCullin spoke of the early over-confidence of the troops, who roamed the streets shooting down dogs for sport, until the strength of the North Vietnamese forces became apparent. The Marine company was led by a 24-year-old officer. There was a lack of experienced non-commissioned officers. At one point the company raced down a street, 'like American cavalry', shooting from the hip and ridiculously exposed. There were terrible casualties. As part of routine mopping up, bunkers and air-raid shelters were approached with the warning cry of 'Fire in the hole'. A grenade would be lobbed in. From one such fired hole a family of wounded Vietnamese civilians emerged. Morale among the soldiers was low. As they looked at their decimated numbers, the civilian dead and the destruction of the ancient cultural capital, the Marines spoke of writing to Congressmen to get America out of Vietnam. A very different mood from two years before, McCullin noted.

His pictures took the Western public to the front-line. A full page of them appeared in *The New York Times* on 28 March 1968. An extraordinary issue of *The Sunday Times Magazine* followed on 24 March. An editorial spoke of the war as 'une guerre sale', in fact as 'one of the dirtiest wars in history'. The story was called 'This is how it is'. There were six spreads, illustrated by 12 photographs with McCullin's captions. Pictures were used large; spread over two pages they measured 33 × 50 cm (13 × 20 inches).

McCullin wrote that 'the most impressive thing was the accuracy of the American shelling. Their ships out at sea were hitting the streets right in front of our positions. And shells from an army base 16 miles (26 kilometres) away were landing 200 yards (180 metres) ahead of us.' However, there was nothing high-tech about the action shown in the photographs. Their nerve roots seem to lie in other and earlier wars. A giant negro hurls a grenade with muscular grace (page 35)—'my Greek javelin thrower' McCullin called him later. A sniper looks up warily. Soldiers stand round a blindfolded civilian suspect. They tend a wounded colleague (page 36). His body is strung with bandoliers, his hands are heavy with jewellery; his spectacles have slipped from his nose and rest on his throat: 'Somebody shouted "Grenade!" We all looked round, saw it lying on the ground behind us and dived

'Somebody shouted "Grenade!" ... This poor bloke didn't move quickly enough ...'

for cover. This poor bloke didn't move quickly enough. I can understand why. There's a moment when you get mesmerized looking at a grenade about to go off. He was left for dead but when we retreated we found him moving.'

Following the pictures in *The Sunday Times Magazine* was an interview-article with McCullin by Francis Wyndham, titled 'A Sort of Madness'. In this McCullin spoke of himself as 'a product of Hitler: I was born in the thirties and bombed in the forties. Then the Hollywood people moved in and started showing me films about violence.' His view of war drew on traditional views of war, but that did not make his photographs less powerful. His pictures wrote the experience of war in headlines. Just a month earlier *The Sunday Times* readership topped 4 million for the first time. McCullin's message was less the terror of war than the reality of it. He discounted its romance: '*The Four Feathers* and all that . . . Vietnam has put an end to the fashion for war. It's feathers all round now, actually.' However, romantic he certainly looked in the inset photograph, resembling a helmeted Marine, camera at neck. Wyndham's text speaks of him as seeming to be 'compulsively attracted by violence and death, and almost unnaturally free of fear. Armed only with a camera, he runs risks in battle perhaps even greater than those of the fighting men.'

Others have vouched for McCullin's courage. Harold Evans, then editor of *The Sunday Times*, spoke of this later: 'Don McCullin's courage is clearly testified to by his photographic images, but in reality never more eloquently than when Nicholas Tomalin was blown up in his car in no-man's-land between the Israeli and Syrian forces during the Yom Kippur war [1973]. As soon as he heard what had happened, McCullin raced down to Tomalin's car, ignoring the warning of Israeli officers, right into the middle of a rocket and rifle area. Having identified the body, he picked up Tomalin's spectacles and ran back to his colleagues and relative safety. Like many brave men, he was terrified. He had dried up completely. When he got back he couldn't speak for minutes.' (Quoted from John le Carré's introduction to *Hearts of Darkness*.)

McCullin covered the front line of the war in Vietnam and showed the vulnerability of men in the ferocious reality of fighting—at a crucial time in the swing of public opinion against the war. He later praised Philip Jones Griffiths' incisive book *Vietnam, Inc* as the largest photographic contribution to ending the war, although he felt the impact of the book was surpassed in some ways by *one* 1968 photograph by Ed Adams: 'He took the head-shooting picture of the Viet Cong suspect which became a turning point.' When McCullin came out of Hué to talk to Fred Emery, ordinary life was carrying on in British newspapers, relieved by such news of the day (*The Times*, 23 January 1968) as the flight of the Beatles to Rishikesh to discover the mind-expanding properties of the East; the cricketer Geoffrey Boycott batted all day in Bridgetown; the Tate Gallery's Roy Lichtenstein exhibition featured a painting which caricatured a comic strip war—*W-H-A-A-M!*

McCullin was briefly in Czechoslovakia in 1968 during the Prague Spring, then to the United States for contrasting stories: 'A Quiet God-Fearing Community' in New England, and a feature on American pro-football titled 'Think Violence or You'll Just Get Killed'. 1969 brought a 'Look at Cuba', 'Genocide' (Indians in Brazil) and a colour series from New Guinea, 'The Savage Awakening', an exotic tribal story. McCullin later said that he was paid £5000, after syndication, for the one day's photographing in New Guinea. There were many other assignments at

Armed only with a camera, he runs risks in battle perhaps even greater than those of fighting men.

58

this time but they are of little consequence beside McCullin's report 'The Accusing Face of Young Biafra' published by *The Sunday Times Magazine* on 1 June 1969.

The Biafran conflict had erupted two years earlier. After Nigeria gained independence from Britain in 1960, the Ibo-speaking peoples in the Eastern region attempted to secede and form the independent state of Biafra between 1967 and 1970. World opinion was divided over the right of their cause. In the war which followed between the Federal Government of Nigeria and Biafra, the Ibo population became penned in a small heartland in south-east Nigeria and cut off from food supplies. Splits in British opinion were reflected at *The Sunday Times* itself, where the newspaper supported the Federal Military Government while the *Magazine* supported Biafra. Richard West wrote an article to accompany McCullin's photographs and argued that the extinction of the 'proud, hard-working, efficient and exuberant state' of Biafra would be a disaster for the whole of Black Africa.

But Biafra was poised on the brink of annihilation when this was published. McCullin's photographs show nothing of the 'efficient' modern state of Biafra. They show the realities of wounded soldiers, starving civilians and dying children. As with the Hué report, this series continues remorselessly from spread to spread— 13 in all (including West's text). They were not the first photographs to detail the suffering inside Biafra but it is likely that they caused most horror and grief, most money to be sent for relief, more vigils in London streets. The photograph of the mother with a baby at her withered breasts (page 33) was printed in the magazine at 33×50 cm (13×20 inch) size. Francis Wyndham and other journalists on the magazine published the McCullin picture as a poster captioned: 'Biafra, The British Government Supports This War. You the Public Could Stop It'. McCullin and his wife flyposted it over Hampstead Garden Suburb in north London, where Prime Minister Harold Wilson had a house. The agony of Biafra continued. In January 1970 the Biafran leaders finally surrendered. McCullin's pictures, which again won the World Press Photographer Award, continue to be widely published and seen, as if they are candles that no one will put out, or stains that cannot be removed. Whenever they appear they have Goya's invisible captions: 'No se puede mirar'—'One cannot look at this'. And 'Yo lo vi'—'I saw this'.

McCullin was assigned to Cambodia when the Vietnam conflict widened in 1969–70. During a battle at Setbo, 16 km (10 miles) south of the capital Phnom Penh, in June 1970 McCullin was wounded by mortar fire. He was able to photograph fellow-wounded in the open lorry which took them to hospital in Phnom Penh (page 42). *The Sunday Times Magazine* published his story on 12 July. The cover was a photograph of paratroopers, beside a jeep, one soldier lying dead or wounded, the rest motionless, alert and obviously under fire. The scene is immaculately exposed and composed, taut as tension wiring. It is, the headline tells us, 'Cambodia: the moment McCullin was hit'. He described the event and the preceding moments in this way. 'I couldn't stay in one place so I leapt out and ran towards a jeep and got down behind it and nobody was moving and the next moment there was an awful clobbering sound that deafened my right ear and I knew something had landed in front of me and I looked down and blood was gushing out of my crotch. A mortar had landed the other side of the jeep. I thought, next time I'm going to get it right in the face, and I started putting my cameras away but I got all the straps muddled up and I thought for Christ's sake, and I ran

McCullin's pictures . . . are candles that no one will put out, stains that cannot be removed.

to a house—the hurt in my legs was terrible, like fire—and I staggered like a drunk with my eyes rolling and fell into a pit full of wounded men.' McCullin's long and extraordinary account is sufficiently terrifying—he had four mortar wounds down the right leg and one just above the knee on the left—but ended when 'a bloke came from nowhere and threw a morphine needle into my left leg and out again', and the lorry got the survivors to safety. He returned to Cambodia to file further reports for his magazine, on the three million refugees there in 1973, and again in 1975 to photograph the make-shift hospitals in Phnom Penh. The city was then under rocket fire from surrounding Khmer Rouge, who took control of the capital and country in April 1975.

McCullin's first trip to India was with Eric Newby for *Town* magazine in 1964 when they produced stories on 'High Life in the Himalayas' and 'Shooting a Princely Line' (how to hunt tigers). He returned to photograph famine in Bihar in 1967 and Mother Theresa's House of the Dying in Calcutta (1970). But his most extensive report was made during the Bangladesh tragedy of 1971 (pages 49, 50, 51, 52 and 53). In March 1971 the East Pakistan Bengalis proclaimed their secession, as the people's republic of Bangladesh, from Punjab-dominated Pakistan. Brutal repression followed, resulting in the flight of millions (estimated as up to 12 millions) of refugees from Bangladesh into neighbouring India. Long picture stories were published by *The Sunday Times Magazine* on 6 June and 5 September 1971. As with so many of his subjects, McCullin's photographs do not minimize the disaster they state.

Those who can look at McCullin's pictures in the magazine with a purely technical eye will see that the illustrations are not ordinary black and white printing. The production people at *The Sunday Times Magazine* evolved a method they call 'four colour black'. A single printing of black would sink into the paper and print grey. McCullin's black and white photographs are printed four colour photogravure. The undercolours of yellow, magenta and cyan boost shadow detail, solid and middle tones. A black key is printed last and sits, holding its shine, on a weight of ink. Light tones are printed with a dot of black. The three colour base is varied for different pictures, sometimes adopting a blueish cast as in the Bangladesh picture of makeshift plastic shelters under monsoon rain (page 49), or towards red in some of the pictures from Hué.

The printing of McCullin's books has been poor (not that it has made much difference to the impact of the photographs) with the exception of the American-produced *Is Anyone Taking Any Notice?* printed by Rapoport, New York. McCullin's own printing—unusually for a top photojournalist—is done by himself, with skill and care. Although he has said that he found W. Eugene Smith's photographs of Minamata somewhat arty considering the tragedy involved ('I hate art, I want my pictures to stink a bit', he said), his own printing seems linked to Smith's by its chiaroscuro effects, its manipulation of light and shade.

In 1979 his photographs of the Middle East and Beirut in particular were used in Jonathan Dimbleby's book *The Palestinians,* and a book on Britain was published as *Homecoming.* This used pictures going back to the beginning of McCullin's career: pictures of coalsearchers (page 11), a set from his series on down-and-outs in London's East End (pages 14 and 15), and a strong collection from his *Sunday Times* report on poverty in Bradford in Yorkshire, but most were specially taken for the book in 1976–78. Possibly the title is a conscious echo of Harold Pinter's

'I hate art, I want my pictures to stink a bit,' he said.

play *The Homecoming,* in which a genial family-gathering turns menacing and nasty, and one review of it was titled 'Bad dream at home'. Pictures of jollity and recreation are mixed with pictures which stare into poverty traps. There are also photographs which seem like pointed allegories—*Caprichos* compared to *Disasters*—as when a street entertainer swallows a mouse, watched with greedy irritation by a cat (pages 16–17), or a mental hospital scene where a file of blind old men are led by a black nurse (page 20).

In 1980, Don McCullin held major exhibitions of his work in London and New York. His earlier work came to the attention of a new generation. His witness to recent history was, he said, to take a new turn. At 45 he wanted to live. He turned his mind to a fashion project for *Tatler* magazine, then a story on British youth for *The Sunday Times.* He began photographing the sea. He promised himself a new start.

However, 1981 found him photographing in El Salvador, where he sustained a broken arm. In 1982 he was barred by the Ministry of Defence from photographing the Falklands War and publicly protested against the decision through a letter to *The Times.* He photographed the Israeli invasion of Beirut in the summer of 1982 and the results are being published as *Beirut: A city in crisis.* In 1983 he complained of the vast press corps hemmed into the same hotel in the same quarter of Beirut and brooded on the difficulties of taking honest pictures as governments take tighter control of access. He's been photographing recently with a newly acquired large-format camera, in Nepal, taking quiet pictures. He says that photography really is limitless and when you agree, he says, 'but just you try'.

Goya has been described as the first modern artist and the forerunner of the best photojournalists. During the French invasion and civil war in his country in 1808–14, Goya was asked to visit his birth place of Saragossa 'to paint the glorious deeds of its citizens'. One plate in the *Disasters of War* shows gallantry—the girl who fired the cannon at the French when all the gunners had been killed—the rest show the anonymous horrors of mutilation and famine. The dramatist Ramon de la Cruz, much admired by Goya, wrote (in opposition to Neoclassical ideals of beauty) that 'There is and has been no greater originality . . . than to copy what can be seen, that is, to portray people, their speech and actions, and their customs.'

That is part of the lineage of photojournalism. In McCullin's case we should add the obvious names—Robert Capa, Gene Smith, and some less obvious ones like Sergeant Len Chetwynd, combat photographer with the British Eighth Army in World War II, and the *Picture Post* photographers like Thurston Hopkins and Bert Hardy. There are differences though. Compared to the way Capa's pictures were published, the production and scale of McCullin's was geared up to a different level. Perhaps it is something like the difference between the songs of Woody Guthrie coming over the radios of America in the 1940s and the sound of Bob Dylan with the full blast of electric power in our own time. There seems little difference between Capa and McCullin in heart, journalistic accomplishment and graphic power—only the power has been turned up.

Technical note

Don McCullin's first camera, bought in 1958, was a Rolleicord twin-lens reflex. However, he soon changed from the 6×6 cm ($2\frac{1}{4} \times 2\frac{1}{4}$ inch) format to 35 mm, beginning with a secondhand Pentax single-lens reflex. He has used 35 mm SLR cameras ever since, sometimes fitted with motor winders to advance the film (not the much faster motor drives).

On assignment he carries two working bodies and two in reserve, carefully protected by foam rubber. He uses just three lenses—28 mm, 35 mm and 135 mm.

He dislikes automatic exposure control cameras and always works with full manual control. He takes exposure readings continually even under combat conditions, using a hand-held meter. As he says, 'I don't want to risk getting killed and then get the exposures all wrong.'

He much prefers shooting black and white than colour and always uses Kodak Tri-X film. Unusually for a top photojournalist, he likes to make his own prints which he does with great skill and care.

Chronology

1935
Born in St Pancras, London.

1944-49
Educated at Primary and Secondary Modern schools in London.

1949
Won Trade Art Scholarship (for drawing ability) to Hammersmith School of Arts and Crafts.

1958
Bought his first camera, a Rolleicord.

1959
First picture story, 'Guv'nors of the Seven Sisters Road', published by *The Observer*.
    Began to work as a freelance photographer.

1961
Married.
    Won press photography award for picture story on the Berlin Wall published in *The Observer*.

1964
First war assignment—covering the civil war in Cyprus for *The Observer*.
    Awarded the Warsaw Gold Medal and the World Press Photographer Award for his Cyprus pictures.
    First visit to Vietnam.

1966
First assignment for *The Sunday Times Magazine*.

1970
Wounded by mortar fire, Cambodia.

1971
Major exhibition, 'The Uncertain Day', at the Kodak Gallery, London.
    Publication of first book, *The Destruction Business*.

1980
Retrospective exhibition at The Victoria & Albert Museum, London, The Side Gallery, Newcastle, and The International Center of Photography, New York.

Bibliography

Books
The Destruction Business, Open Gate Books, London, 1971.
Is Anyone Taking Any Notice?, The M.I.T. Press, Cambridge, Massachussetts, 1973.
Homecoming, Macmillan, London, 1979.
The Palestinians, Macmillan, 1979.
Hearts of Darkness, Secker & Warburg, London, 1980.
Beirut: A city of crisis, New English Library, London, 1983.

Anthologies
The Concerned Photographer 2, New York and London, 1972.
Images of Man: the photographs of W. Eugene Smith, Bruce Davidson, Cornell Capa and Don McCullin (a teaching guide and tape/slide programme), New York, 1972.

Films
Beautiful, Beautiful, on Cornell Capa, Larry Burrows, W. Eugene Smith, Bruce Davidson and Don McCullin, directed by John Irvin, BBC TV, 1969.
Just One More War, directed by Jane Bokova, Associated Television, UK, 1977.

Magazine portfolios
Photography, June 1959.
Camera, Lucerne, June 1963.
Camera Owner, April and June 1967.
Infinity, USA, April 1968.
Album, No. 11, 1970.
The Mainichi Graphic, Tokyo, 23 August 1970.
Camera Mainichi, Tokyo, September 1970.
Zoom, Paris, January/February 1972.
Zoom, Paris, March/April 1972.
Photo, Paris, 1972.
The Image, No. 12, 1973.
Photo, Paris, September 1974.

Index of
photographs

Author

Mark Haworth-Booth was educated at the Universities of Cambridge and Edinburgh. He has worked since 1970 at the Victoria and Albert Museum in London, where he is in charge of the National Collection of the Art of Photography. He directed Donald McCullin's major retrospective exhibition at the V & A in 1980. Other important shows he has arranged include 'The Compassionate Camera: Dustbowl Pictures' in 1973; 'The Land: 20th Century Landscape Photographs', selected by Bill Brandt (1975); and 'The Guide to Early Photographic Processes' with Brian Coe and 'Personal Choice: A Celebration of 20th Century Photographs', both at the V & A in 1983.

First published in 1983 by
William Collins Sons & Co Ltd

London · Glasgow · Sydney
Auckland · Johannesburg

© 1982 Gruppo Editoriale Fabbri S.p.A., Milan

ISBN 0 00 411935 5

Typesetting by Chambers Wallace, London
Printed in Italy